YOU CHOOSE

BOLD RESCUE OF THE FORGOTTEN 500

INTERACTIVE WORLD WAR II MISSIONS

by Allison Lassieur

CAPSTONE PRESS
a capstone imprint

Published by Capstone Press, an imprint of Capstone
1710 Roe Crest Drive, North Mankato, Minnesota 56003
capstonepub.com

Library of Congress Cataloging-in-Publication Data
is available on the Library of Congress website.

ISBN: 9798875244490 (hardcover)
ISBN: 9798875244469 (paperback)
ISBN: 9798875244476 (ebook PDF)

Summary: You are taking part in Operation Halyard, one of the most ambitious secret missions of World War II. In this interactive adventure, YOU CHOOSE the paths that will lead you and others to freedom or spell your doom!

Editorial Credits
Editor: Alison Deering; Designer: Bobbie Nuytten;
Media Researcher: Svetlana Zhurkin; Production Specialist: Katy LaVigne

Image Credits
Alamy: VTR, 64; Associated Press: dpa/picture-alliance/Archiv/Fotoarchiv für Zeitgeschichte, 99; Bridgeman Images: Scherl/© SZ Photo, 83; DVIDS: NARA, 50, Photo courtesy of the National Museum of the U.S. Air Force, 4, U.S. Air Force photo by R.J. Oriez, 17, U.S. Air Force photo by Staff Sgt. Emily Farnsworth, 108 (top), U.S. Air Force photo by Tech. Sgt. Ryan Crane, 104; Getty Images: Fiona Miller, 68, LifeJourneys, 22, Stocktrek Images/Mark Stevenson, 76; NARA: U.S. Air Force, 35, 79, 101, 108 (bottom); Shutterstock: Buch and Bee (airplane emblem), 5 and throughout, Czerep rubaszny, 6–7 (base map), dragana serbia, 24, Ensuper, 8, 12, 40, 74, 102, Fotokon, 88, George Trumpeter, cover (bottom), 58, jollys_art (old paper), cover and throughout, Pablo Caridad (paper file), 1 and throughout, Valentin Agapov (folder), back cover and throughout, Wirestock Creators, cover (top); SuperStock: Universal Images/HUM Images, 96; Wikimedia: Aleksandar Simic, 32, Vanilice, 70

Printed and bound in China. 6461

TABLE OF CONTENTS

B-24 bombers destroy oil fields controlled by Nazi Germany.

ABOUT YOUR ADVENTURE

YOU are about to experience Operation Halyard, one of the most ambitious—and secret—rescues of World War II. You could be a gunner on an American B-24 bomber, sent to destroy German oil refineries. Or you might be a young radio operator, freshly recruited for a secret mission to rescue American crewmen trapped in Nazi-occupied Yugoslavia. Or maybe you are a war-weary Yugoslavian soldier, ordered to protect any stranded American crewman you find.

Wherever you are, whatever path YOU CHOOSE could mean the difference between survival or death for you and others. Follow the directions at the bottom of the page. The decisions you make will determine your fate.

Turn the page to begin your adventure.

OPERATION HALYARD

Operation Halyard was the largest and most successful rescue mission of World War II. The goal of the mission was to find and rescue hundreds of missing American pilots who had been shot down by the German air force while on bombing missions. The pilots were trapped behind enemy lines somewhere in the mountains of Yugoslavia. For months, the Allied forces did not know the men were there. When United States officers found out, they began planning a rescue mission with help from Yugoslavian soldiers and spies from the Office of Strategic Servies.

When:

Operation Halyard was launched on August 9, 1944, from U.S. air bases in Bari and Brindisi, Italy. The U.S. 15th Air Force, designated as the 1st Air Crew Rescue Unit, was assigned to the rescue. They sent planes to Pranjani, Yugoslavia (now Serbia), where the men had gathered. The rescue continued for the next five months. By December, 432 American airmen, plus another 80 Allied personnel, were safely out.

SOVIET UNION

Key Terms

Allies—the United Kingdom, the United States, the Soviet Union, China, and France

Chetniks—a band of Yugoslavian soldiers who helped rescue surviving American pilots when their planes went down; the Chetniks led Americans to villages, where civilians hid the pilots from German forces.

Luftwaffe—German air force

Nazi—a member of a political party led by Adolf Hitler; the Nazis ruled Germany from 1933 to 1945.

Office of Strategic Services (OSS)—a U.S. intelligence agency that functioned during WWII; the OSS helped coordinate spy activity behind enemy lines.

35
30
700
20
40
500
60
80
300
100
9
8
1
7
6
5
4
3
100%
100
80

Chapter 1

TRAPPED BEHIND ENEMY LINES

The year is 1944, and World War II is raging. Nazi armies—under the command of Germany's leader, Adolph Hitler—have conquered or destroyed much of Europe. U.S. Army commanders want to cripple the Nazi armies and defeat Hitler. Slowly, they've pushed the Nazi armies out of parts of Europe, but the Germans still control many countries. Allied commanders need to come up with a plan that will destroy Hitler's armies for good.

One way to do so is to destroy German oil refineries—factories responsible for turning crude oil into gasoline and other fuel. The Germans control many refineries in Romania—the ones in Ploesti, Romania, supply one third of the army's fuel. If these refineries are destroyed, Hitler's bombers, tanks, and other war weapons would have no fuel to run.

There is only one problem. These refineries are ferociously defended by Germany's deadly air force, the Luftwaffe.

U.S. commanders decide to order the missions anyway. Wave after wave of American bombers attack the refineries in Romania. The Luftwaffe shoot down dozens of bombers and kill hundreds of American soldiers. Hundreds more survive by parachuting into neighboring Yugoslavia.

Now the men are trapped in German-occupied territory, surrounded by Nazi forces with no way to escape. Help comes from an unlikely source—the people of Yugoslavia. Most of the villagers in Yugoslavia hate the Germans. They are eager for the Americans to win the war, and they want to help.

U.S. commanders come up with an ambitious plan to rescue the survivors—Operation Halyard. They will instruct spies from the OSS to find the men and send rescue planes into Yugoslavia to pick them up. But they must do it without the Nazi armies noticing.

Can hundreds of men be rescued without Hitler and his armies finding out? It will take the efforts—and lives—of many people, including American army officers, OSS spies, and the Yugoslavian people. Do you have the courage to survive behind enemy lines or risk death to save American crewmen?

To be a member of an American bomber crew shot down behind enemy lines in Yugoslavia, turn to page 13.

To be a radio operator recruited by the OSS to find survivors in the Nazi-infested countryside, turn to page 41.

To be a Yugoslavian Chetnik soldier helping Americans escape despite the terrible danger, turn to page 75.

Chapter 2

BAIL OUT! WE'RE GOING DOWN!

You're filled with determination, excitement, and fear as your B-24 bomber plane zooms through the dark skies over Romania. When the U.S. entered the war in 1941, you couldn't wait to join the U.S. Army Air Force. When you finally enlisted, you trained to be a gunner, firing machine guns at enemy planes from bomber aircraft.

Today's mission is to destroy German oil refineries in Ploesti. But the mission is a dangerous one—the Luftwaffe patrols the air space above the city. They won't hesitate to shoot down an American plane.

Thankfully, your B-24 bomber has a well-trained crew—a pilot, copilot, navigator,

Turn the page.

six gunners, and a bombardier who aims for the targets and drops the bombs. Even though it is a large plane, it is cramped inside. Between the bombs, equipment, instruments, and nine other people, you barely have any space to move. You squeeze into your seat and try not to think of the danger ahead.

After several hours of flying, you're at Ploesti. Roy, the pilot, shouts above the roar of the engines. "Get into position, boys!"

Nervously, you swing your gun into position, aiming out a window in the middle of the plane. Jimmy, the bombardier, calculates the target's position. Then he activates the mechanism that drops the bombs. One by one, the bombs roll out and disappear into the night. You see red, fiery explosions far below.

"It's a hit!" Jimmy cries.

The mission is a success! The refineries you were sent to cripple have been destroyed or severely damaged. As your bomber turns for the long flight home, dozens of planes suddenly fill the sky. It's the Luftwaffe! They're heading toward you with sickening speed.

You hear the *ping-ping-ping* of bullets hitting metal. Your plane shudders and tilts crazily, throwing you all to the floor.

"We've been hit!" Roy shouts. "Hang on!"

The B-24 starts dropping quickly. Roy fights with the controls.

"I can't hold her in the air much longer!" he shouts. "Bail out!"

That's when you see blood covering Roy's shoulder. He's hurt.

"I'll keep the plane up long enough for everyone to get out!" Roy yells. "Then I'll go!"

You have been trained for parachute jumping. The parachutes are too bulky to

Turn the page.

wear in the plane, so you grab your chute from the wall and clip it on. The others quickly do the same, then jump out of the open hatch of the plane. You watch as they release their parachutes and float away into the darkness. Soon, you and Roy are the only ones left.

"Go!" he yells. "I'll be fine!"

With that injury, there's no way Roy can bail out on his own. Do you risk your life to save Roy too? Or do you save yourself?

To stay on the plane, go to page 17.

To jump out of the plane, turn to page 26.

"I'm not leaving without you!" you shout.

The plane drops closer to the ground as a Luftwaffe screams past. It shoots, and the plane jerks hard. Red flames burst from one engine. If you don't jump now, it will be too late.

"We have to go!" you shout.

You clip on Roy's parachute, then drag him to the open hatch. There is no time to waste—you jump.

Turn the page.

The cold night air hits you like a thousand knives. Quickly, you pull the cords on the parachutes, and the fabric billows out, carrying you both safely to the ground. You land in a wide farm field ringed by forest.

Moving fast, you pull Roy to the cover of the trees and lay him down gently. The pilot has lost a lot of blood. You reach for your first aid kit. Every crew member carries one in his flight suit. But yours is gone! You search Roy's pockets, but his is missing too.

Surely one of the other crewmen has his kit. You need to find them. They jumped only a few seconds before you did. That means they probably landed nearby. But you don't want to leave Roy alone—he is conscious but barely.

To stay with Roy, go to page 19.

To look for the others, turn to page 21.

"I won't leave you behind, buddy," you promise Roy.

Staring at the pilot's grim expression, you know you really need that first aid kit. But it's pitch black, and you don't know where you are. Even worse, the area is crawling with German troops. If they find you, you're dead. The best option is to stay put until dawn. Then you'll be able to find the others.

Soon, you're asleep. Hours later, you're jerked awake by a hard kick to your side. German soldiers have surrounded you. Panic and fear washes over you when you see Roy's body. You can't tell if he was shot or if he died from his wounds. It doesn't matter now.

The German soldiers take aim. You can only hope someone tells your family what happened to you. The sound of gunshots is followed by a searing pain, then the world goes dark.

Turn the page.

When you open your eyes, it's daylight. Your whole body is on fire with pain. The Gemans are gone. They must have thought you were dead.

You hear voices, then a big man with a bushy beard leans down, staring at you. He gently pours water in your mouth, and you greedily slurp it. Then he shouts, and many strong hands lift you into a splintery wooden cart. The man pats your shoulder as the cart jerks forward. You don't know who these people are or where they're taking you, but you're alive and safe—for now.

THE END

To follow another path, turn to page 11.
To learn more about Operation Halyard, turn to page 103.

"You need help," you say to Roy. "I'm going to look for the others. I'll be back quickly."

The pilot nods in understanding. He's pale and covered in blood. You don't have much time.

You scan the area, trying to figure out where the others landed. Finally, you determine which way the plane was going when they bailed out. You set off in that direction, but it's very dark, and you have trouble keeping your bearings. After some time, you hear voices in the distance.

At first, your heart leaps with hope—maybe it's your crewmates! But it could also be German soldiers patrolling the area. They must have seen the air battle and will be looking for American survivors. Maybe you should hide and wait.

To go toward the voices, turn to page 22.

To hide and wait, turn to page 24.

"Here I am!" you shout.

The voices stop. Then they start shouting and running toward you. Your heart sinks as you realize the terrible mistake you've made. They are German soldiers.

One German pulls a gun, and they haul you through the woods to a larger patrol. They argue for some time. You don't speak German, but it is not difficult to understand that they're trying to decide whether or not to kill you.

Nazi soldiers on patrol

Finally, the soldiers come to a decision. The leader ties your hands, and they march you out of the woods. For the next weeks they force you to march to a prisoner-of-war camp. Hundreds of U.S. airmen are already there. You'll spend the rest of the war trapped in the camp. But at least you're alive.

Every day you wonder what happened to Roy. Did he die of his injuries, or was he found and killed by German soldiers? Maybe he was rescued. You will probably never know. If you survive, you vow to find Roy's family and tell them of the brave sacrifice he made to save you and the rest of the crew.

THE END

To follow another path, turn to page 11.
To learn more about Operation Halyard, turn to page 103.

You have to find a place to hide. The area is filled with German camps and patrols. If they find you, they will kill you.

You head for some trees. As you search for a hiding place, you become aware of pain in your stomach. Glancing down, you see a dark patch on your shirt widening at an alarming rate—blood. In all the commotion and concern for Roy, you didn't realize you were wounded too.

Dizziness and exhaustion wash over you. You manage to crawl under some thick underbrush and lay there, panting with pain. You struggle to stay conscious and wonder what will happen to Roy and the others. Then you think about your family back home. Your mother's kind face is your last thought as you close your eyes and sink into darkness.

German soldiers find your body and bury it in a shallow grave. Back home, the Army lists you as "missing in action"—no one ever knows what happened to you.

THE END

To follow another path, turn to page 11.
To learn more about Operation Halyard, turn to page 103.

Holding your breath, you hurl yourself out of the plane into the inky darkness. The cold air cuts painfully through your lungs. You pull the cord on your parachute, feeling the fabric pull as it catches the air.

A few seconds later, you land hard on your side. You feel a loud *crunch,* and searing pain shoots up your arm.

But there's no time to be injured. You unbuckle the parachute and bury it as best you can. You don't want the Luftwaffe to spot the huge white parachute from the sky. It would lead the Germans directly to your location.

When you finally get the parachute hidden, you glimpse a light bobbing toward you. Your heart stops. It could be German soldiers! Or it might be one of your crewmates looking for you. What do you do?

To hide from the light, go to page 27.

To approach the light, turn to page 31.

You're not going to risk capture or death, so you head toward a line of trees. The ground is wet and uneven, and you trip several times. It's all you can do not to scream from the pain each time.

Finally, you stumble into the woods. You walk until you feel like you can't take another step. All you want to do is rest. But German soldiers might find you if you don't keep moving.

To rest anyway, turn to page 28.

To keep going, turn to page 30.

You can't go any farther. You tuck yourself beside a fallen log and pass out from pain and exhaustion. You have no idea how long you've been out when a voice jars you awake.

"Hey, buddy, are you dead?"

It's Jimmy, the bombardier from your plane. Your crewmates are standing in a circle around you. Even Roy is here! They're all dirty and bloody, but they're alive.

A tall Yugoslavian steps into the circle.

"This is Josif," Jimmy says. "He's a Chetnik soldier with General Draza Mihailovic's army. He speaks English."

Josif nods. "I have orders from General Mihailovic to find downed American soldiers."

"He's taking us to a village called Pranjani," Jimmy says. "The army is planning a rescue!"

Your head is spinning, and you feel cold and hot all at once.

Jimmy puts a hand to your forehead. "You're burning up." He looks at Josif. "He won't make it to Pranjani."

Josif nods."There's a village about a day's walk from here. I will take the others there and come back with medicine and a wagon."

"I'll stay here with him," Jimmy offers.

Quickly, the others say their goodbyes, then they're gone.

"Get some sleep," Jimmy says, wrapping his flight jacket around your shoulders. "I'll take care of you, buddy."

Gratefully, you lie down and close your eyes. You don't know what's going to happen next. But for now, you're safe and on the way to being rescued.

THE END

To follow another path, turn to page 11.
To learn more about Operation Halyard, turn to page 103.

You force yourself to keep moving, but the world starts spinning. You bend over a fallen log and throw up—onto a sleeping German soldier!

The other man yells and jumps to his feet. For a moment, you freeze. Then both of you reach for your knives and lunge.

The fight is brief. When it is over, you realize there is blood on your flight suit. And it is not the German's—it's yours.

You slide to the ground and lean against the log. Oddly, there is no pain. It's a relief to know that death doesn't hurt as the world dims, then disappears forever.

THE END

To follow another path, turn to page 11.
To learn more about Operation Halyard, turn to page 103.

You approach the light and encounter an older Yugoslavian woman holding a lantern. To your surprise, she gives you a huge hug! You follow her to a cozy farmhouse. She splints your arm, feeds you, and gives you a place to sleep.

The next morning, a Yugoslavian Chetnik solider is waiting. He motions for you to follow him. The woman nods and gives you a comforting smile.

You nod in agreement and follow the soldier out the door. You are beginning to understand that these people aren't planning to hurt you or turn you in to the Nazis. As you leave, the woman presses a chunk of bread into your hand. You did not expect such kindness, but you're grateful for it.

For days, you trudge through the Yugoslavian countryside. One afternoon, a large village comes into view.

Turn the page.

Someone shouts your name. You can hardly believe your eyes—it's Jimmy! Soon you're surrounded by your crewmates. Even Roy is here! You're overjoyed to see them alive.

"What is this place?" you ask.

"Pranjani," Jimmy replies. "General Mihailovic, the leader of the Yugoslavian Army, ordered his men to find American survivors and bring us here. Mihailovic and his soldiers want to beat the Germans as bad as we do. Three OSS officers just parachuted in. They're working with Mihailovic to plan some kind of rescue."

Yugoslavian Army leader Draza Mihailovic

Lieutenant George Musulin asks to see you. He is one of the OSS agents and the leader of the rescue mission.

"When the army found out you boys were here, we knew we had to get you out," he says. "We're going to fly everyone out. We need to build an airstrip, but we have to be very careful not to alert the Germans. If they find out, they'll bomb us into oblivion."

He looks at your arm. "If you're injured, you're exempt from airstrip duty. Your job is to be strong enough to board that rescue plane."

You should take care of your arm. But you also want to be of use to the rescue effort.

To rest, turn to page 34.

To help with the airstrip, turn to page 36.

You report to the makeshift field hospital. By now, you're feeling feverish. The medic examines you, and frowns.

"It looks like your arm is infected," he says.

The days pass in a blur of pain. You drift in and out of consciousness. Jimmy, Roy, and the others take turns sitting with you. One night, they hustle in and wrap you in blankets.

"The rescue planes are here," Jimmy says.

You are barely conscious when they load you into a cargo plane with other sick and injured men. You wake up in a clean, bright hospital in Italy.

"Welcome back, soldier," the nurse says. "Doc says you've been discharged. You're going home."

That's good news. Before you ship out, all your crewmates visit you in the hospital. You're overjoyed to see them! They're all going

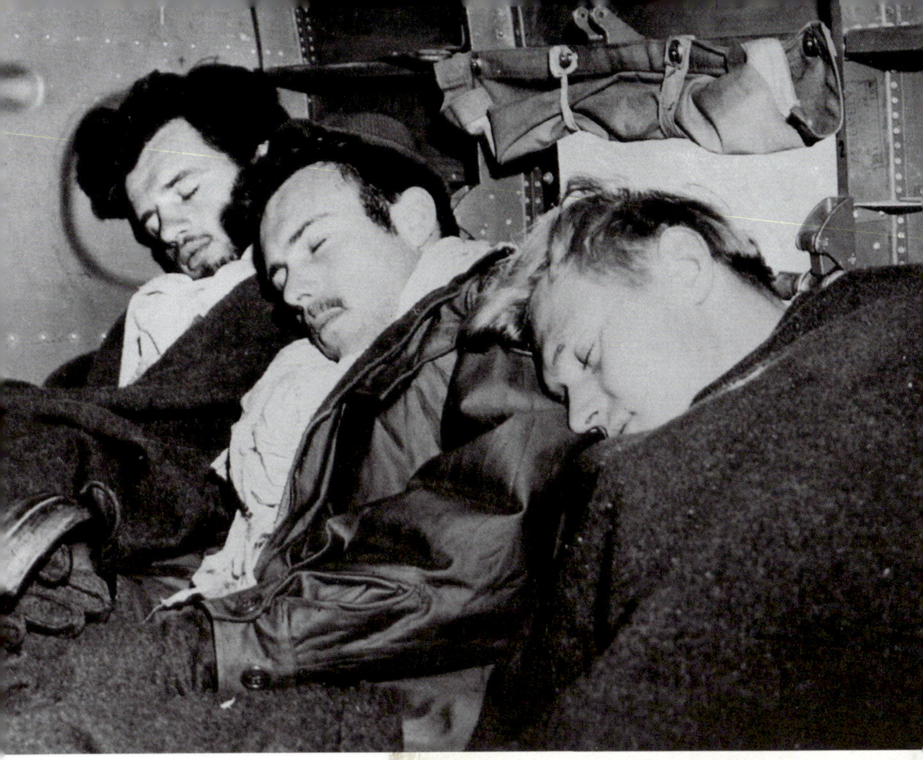

American airmen rest on their flight to Italy after being rescued in Yugoslavia.

back to the war, and they came to say goodbye. You don't know if you'll ever see them again, but you'll always remember Jimmy, Roy, and the kind Yugoslavian people who helped you.

THE END

To follow another path, turn to page 11.
To learn more about Operation Halyard, turn to page 103.

You're determined to help. The next evening, you and hundreds of other Americans, Chetnik soldiers, and local villagers trek to a mountain field. Huge boulders dot the area, but you don't see any tools or equipment.

"We're building it with our bare hands," Jimmy explains, handing you a farmer's hoe.

For the next six days, the airstrip takes shape. Some cut down trees while others break boulders and level out the bumpy land. Work crews use wooden oxcarts to haul away the dirt and debris.

You do your best with your injured arm. It's backbreaking work, and your hands are covered with painful blisters.

Luftwaffe planes constantly fly overhead. When they appear, everyone hides in the nearby woods. Every day, you expect an attack. Thankfully, none come.

The Germans must think this is just another farmer's field. You hope it stays that way.

When the airstrip is done, Lieutenant Musulin radios main command. They reply that they are sending six C-47 cargo planes. The planes will be coming that night.

After dark, the men set up fire pots along the airstrip so the rescue pilots can see where to land. The whine of engines fills the air as cargo planes approach.

Soon, the C-47s are safely on the ground. But there are only four planes, not six. That means dozens of men won't be leaving tonight. Because of your injury, you are at the top of the list to go. You could get on a plane. Or you can let a more critcally injured man take your place.

To board the plane, turn to page 38.

To stay behind, turn to page 39.

Musulin says that more planes will arrive soon for the others, so you get onboard. Villagers surround the planes, cheering and waving goodbye.

You want to thank these kind people, but you don't have anything to give them. Finally, you decide to give your heavy flight jacket and sturdy army boots to a villager. Other airmen give their jackets and shoes away too.

One by one, the C-47s take off into the dark night. Luckily, the darkness also prevents the Germans from seeing the rescue. You all make it safely to the U.S. Army base in Brindisi, Italy.

There, doctors reset your arm, but the damage is permanent. They discharge you from the army, but you feel only relief. You're going home for good.

THE END

To follow another path, turn to page 11.
To learn more about Operation Halyard, turn to page 103.

You decide to wait. Over the next few hours, more rescue planes arrive—along with squads of American fighter planes. The fighters attack the German camps, keeping them distracted so the rescue planes can get away.

You're in the last group to leave. As you are boarding the C-47, you unlace your boots and hand them to a villager. It's all you have to give, and you want to thank them for all they've done. The man embraces you in return.

As the plane lifts off, you think back to everything that has happened. You're grateful to everyone who played a part in your rescue. You can't wait to get back into the fight to defeat the Germans and win this war.

THE END

To follow another path, turn to page 11.
To learn more about Operation Halyard, turn to page 103.

35
30
700
20
40
500
60
300
80
100
9
8
1
7
3
6
5
4
100%
100
80

Chapter 3

DANGEROUS SEARCH FOR SURVIVORS

When the United States entered World War II in 1941, you were still a kid in high school. Now it's 1944, and you're a new army volunteer, fresh out of boot camp, where you trained as a radio operator.

One afternoon, someone from the Office of Strategic Services shows up at boot camp. You've heard of the OSS. It is the American spy service, and they are looking for a radio operator.

"What does an OSS radio operator do?" you ask.

"You'll go with other OSS agents on secret missions and parachute into enemy territory," the OSS agent replies.

Turn the page.

"You'll use the radio to send top-secret information such as enemy troop locations."

Being an OSS spy radio operator sounds exciting. You say yes on the spot.

Now, two weeks later, you are finished with boot camp and on a military plane somewhere over eastern Europe. You and two other OSS agents, Lieutenant George Musulin and Master Sergeant Mike Rajacich, make up the rescue team heading toward your first mission—Operation Halyard.

Musulin is the mission leader. He has been to Yugoslavia and is friends with the Yugoslavian Army commander, Draza Mihailovic. Rajacich speaks the local language and will be the translator. Your job is to establish radio contact with the American base in Italy.

The team will parachute into Yugoslavia and begin the search for the American crewmen. You have information that they are gathering in the mountain village of Pranjani. But none of you know exactly where that is. What you *do* know is that there will be many Nazi soldiers between you and the village. You have to make contact with Chetnik soldiers who can safely lead you to Pranjani.

"We're over the jump point!" the pilot finally shouts. "Good luck!"

You had only two training sessions on parachute jumping at boot camp. Now it's time to remember what to do. Heart beating with fear, you grab the radio case and leap out of the plane. Once you're clear, you pull the cord on your paracute.

When you're all safely on the ground, Musulin and Rajacich hide the parachutes while you set up the radio. Its powerful signal can travel 500 miles.

Turn the page.

Your first task is to contact the OSS base in Cairo, Egypt, to let them know you arrived. There's only one problem: the Germans will likely hear the transmission. You'll have to move fast, before they can pinpoint your location.

You try to send the message, but all you hear is static.

"I can't get a signal here," you say. "We need to move higher up the mountain."

"There's a German camp that way," Musulin replies. "I'm not sure we should risk it."

Rajacich scans the sky. "All this cloud cover could be blocking the signal," he says. "When the sky clears up you can try again."

To keep trying where you are, go to page 45.

To move to higher ground, turn to page 53.

You decide to stay put—where it's safer. When the clouds clear you try again. Suddenly you hear the roar of airplane engines. Your worst nightmare comes true as several German air force bombers—the Luftwaffe—appear in the sky and open fire.

You shout for help, but Musulin and Rajacich have disappeared. You drop the radio and run. Every time you find a good hiding place, the Luftwaffe discover you. They shoot, and you run again, trying to stay out of firing range.

The Luftwaffe pilots chase you until nightfall. Finally, they give up and fly away. You collapse, exhausted. That's when you notice the throbbing pain in your foot. Your ankle is so swollen that you can't get your boot off.

As you wonder what to do, a large, bearded man appears. He eyes you suspiciously.

Turn the page.

You show him the U.S. insignia on your uniform, and the Yugoslavian man's eyes light up in recognition. He motions for you to follow him, but you shake your head and point to your foot.

The man nods in understanding. He carefully cuts off the boot, relieving the awful pressure and pain a little. Then he helps you up and takes you to his nearby farm.

He wraps your ankle, then his wife offers you water and food. Greedily, you gulp it down as several children watch, wide-eyed.

You're still eating when a commotion erupts outside. It's a group of German officers! The Luftwaffe must have told them where you were. You only have seconds to decide whether you'll escape or hide.

To escape, go to page 47.

To hide, turn to page 48.

You sneak out the back door and head into the forest as fast as your broken ankle will carry you. Finally, the pain becomes so bad that you can't walk any farther.

At first, you hope the farmer will find you. But as the hours turn into days, you realize no one is coming.

You're dizzy with thirst. You hoist yourself up and try to walk. Every step is horribly painful, but you keep going until you reach the farm. There, you stop in horror.

The buildings are piles of charred wood. There's no sign of the farmer and his family. The Germans destroyed it all. Slowly, you slide to the ground and close your eyes. The smell of smoke stings your nose as you fall unconscious and die of dehydration.

THE END

To follow another path, turn to page 11.
To learn more about Operation Halyard, turn to page 103.

You scramble under the bed. The Germans are pounding on the door now, and the farmer hurries to open it.

From your hiding place, you see heavy black boots as they stomp through the house. One officer pauses next to the bed. He's so close you can see the mud stains on his boots.

You close your eyes and hold your breath. If he finds you, you're dead.

After a moment, the German spins on his heel, and the boots storm out of the house. You let out your breath with a *woosh* and crawl out from under the bed. Your whole body is trembling. That was a very close call.

The farmer offers the bed to you. A night's rest in a real bed would be wonderful. But the Germans could return. Maybe you should hide in the barn instead.

To stay in the house, go to page 49.

To sleep in the barn, turn to page 50.

It's not likely the Germans will come back—they've already searched the house once. Gratefully, you accept the farmer's kind offer. The family settles down in the loft. You sink into the soft mattress and instantly fall asleep.

But in the middle of the night, you bolt upright. Something woke you—but what?

Suddenly, there is a loud *CRASH!* A German stick grenade flies through the window, shattering the glass. The grenade explodes in a fiery ball, filling the house with flames and smoke.

The Germans must have seen you after all! You don't have time to move before flames engulf the bed. The last thing you hear are the family's screams as fire engulfs the house.

THE END

To follow another path, turn to page 11.
To learn more about Operation Halyard, turn to page 103.

It's safer for everyone if you sleep in the barn. You burrow into the sweet-smelling hay. It's not long before you're snoring peacefully.

Then, in the middle of the night, you jerk awake. Did you hear something? But the world is quiet. The farmer's cow shifts softly in her stall. You relax and settle back into the hay.

CRASH! Several German soldiers are throwing stick grenades through the farmhouse windows! The house explodes in a ball of flames. It is too late for the farmer

A German soldier hurls a stick grenade.

and his family. You can't save them. All you can do now is save yourself.

You limp into the woods, praying that the Germans don't notice. Every step sends terrible pain up your leg. Then, rough hands grab you in the dark. You struggle until someone else puts you in a chokehold.

"Shhh!" a harsh voice hisses.

It's Musulin and Rajacich. Instantly, you stop fighting, and they let go.

"We've been dodging German patrols all night," Musulin tells you quietly.

"Then we saw a bunch of officers head straight here," Rajacich adds in a whisper. "We figured maybe they had captured you, so we followed them."

"Good thing we did," Musulin says.

You nod silently. You are so relieved they found you!

Turn the page.

Together, the two men carry you far away from the horrors you just witnessed. At dawn, you come upon a small village guarded by Yugoslavian Chetnik soldiers. Once you're fed and rested, the soldiers take you to Pranjani. Sure enough, hundreds of Americans are here. Musulin orders you to a medic.

"When you're fixed up, get back here," Musulin orders. "We need to make radio contact with the base and coordinate this rescue. It's going to be big. No one has any idea there are so many guys to get out."

As the medic is wrapping your leg, all you can think about is the farmer and his family—dead because they helped you. You will never forget them. You vow to help as many Americans—and villagers—as you can, until the Germans are crushed and this war is over.

THE END

To follow another path, turn to page 11.
To learn more about Operation Halyard, turn to page 103.

After a long, hard climb, you reach a clear area and set up the radio. You type out the message and wait. The radio crackles to life and a reply comes through! The base acknowledges your message and confirms your location. You're relieved that the OSS base in Cairo knows you're alive. But you end the transmission as quickly as possible so the Nazis can't track the signal.

"Great job," Musulin says. "Our orders are to make contact with the Chetnik army. They'll take us to Pranjani, where our men are."

As you're packing up the radio, a squad of bombers appear in the sky. The Luftwaffe! You have to get out of there—fast.

You see two paths. The left winds around a hill and disappears. The path on your right climbs higher. But which one leads to safety?

To choose the path to the left, turn to page 54.

To choose the path on your right, turn to page 55.

You drop the radio and run for your life, Musulin and Rajacich close behind you, as the bombers open fire. The path takes a sharp turn, and you find yourself at the edge of a huge mountain cliff.

You're running too frantically to stop. You lose your footing and slide on the loose rocks and dirt.

Musulin grabs your shirt and tries to pull you back, but you're running too fast. The world drops out from under you as you go over the edge.

Oddly, your mind is clear as you plummet through the air. *I thought I would die from a German bullet*, is your final thought.

THE END

To follow another path, turn to page 11.
To learn more about Operation Halyard, turn to page 103.

The radio isn't worth your life, so you leave it behind and follow Musulin and Rajacich up the steep, rocky path. For hours, the Luftwaffe chase you up the mountain. The three of you desperately hide under trees and behind boulders, trying to lose the Germans.

Eventually, the bombers give up and fly away. But now it's dark, and you're lost on top of a mountain. The temperature drops, and snow begins to fall. None of you are dressed for cold weather. The frigid wind burns your skin. You lose feeling in your feet.

Just as you can't go any further, you see tiny points of light in the darkness. A village!

You stumble through the snow to a small house. Musulin knocks frantically, and a man answers. When he sees you are Americans, he pulls you inside. Soon you're eating hot soup beside a warm, crackling fire.

Turn the page.

Musulin and Rajacich speak the local language, so they talk to the man for a long time. You doze by the fire until Musulin turns to you.

"Nikola wants to help us, but he doesn't know anything about a large group of Americans," he says. "He does know of other American pilots who are hiding from the Germans and need help." Then Musulin frowns. "We'll have to sneak through a German checkpoint to get to them, though."

Rescuing other pilots is not part of Operation Halyard. But these men need help too. Do you risk your life trying to get to them? Or do you follow orders and find the American pilots you were sent to rescue?

To risk a new plan, go to page 57.

To keep looking for the larger group, turn to page 63.

"We've lost all our gear, and we don't know where our airmen are," you say. "But if we can save *someone*, at least we'll have done something."

Musulin nods. "We may have escaped the Luftwaffe for now, but they know we're here," he says gravely. "Operation Halyard has been compromised."

"There's a good chance the Nazis could follow us to Pranjani and alert their ground troops to that location," Rajacich adds. "We have to abandon Operaton Halyard for now and locate the hiding American pilots. Then we'll figure out how to get us all out."

"Some of the German guards can be bribed to let you pass the checkpoint," Nikola says. "I can take you."

Musulin shakes Nikola's hand. "I know how dangerous this is for you," he says. "Thank you for your help."

Turn the page.

"Yugoslavians want Nazis out of our country," he replies. "We will help Americans any way we can."

The next day, Nikola takes some coins and disappears. When he returns, he's smiling.

"The guards accepted the bribe," he says. "But you must go tonight."

Around midnight, Nikola leads you to the checkpoint. A large building looms in the darkness. Two German soldiers stand guard at the entrance to a bridge.

A German World War II era checkpoint

Carefully you step toward the bridge. The guards see you. Will they let you pass?

After a moment, the guards turn their backs. They're letting you through!

Heart pounding, you dash across the bridge. When you get halfway across, you take a breath. Almost there.

Suddenly a huge spotlight switches on, flooding the whole bridge with harsh light. You freeze, terrified. Did the guards betray you? Did someone else see you cross?

You and the others draw your weapons as angry German shouting echos across the bridge. Machine gun fire explodes all around. You have seconds to decide what to do.

To run across the bridge, turn to page 60.

To return fire, turn to page 61.

You run for your life across the bridge. You're only a few yards away from safety when a searing pain rips through your back, then your leg. You've been shot.

You crumple against the bridge rail, breathing hard. You knew that getting shot would hurt, but you had no idea how much.

The world seems to slow down as you're shot again, this time in the shoulder. You can't hold onto the rail any longer. Strangely, you feel calm, knowing death is coming. Before another shot can come, you let go and plunge into the black, rushing river far below.

THE END

To follow another path, turn to page 11.
To learn more about Operation Halyard, turn to page 103.

You're not going down without a fight! You shoot at the spotlight. It shatters, plunging the bridge into darkness once again. Now it's time to run!

German soldiers chase the three of you through the forest. Your lungs burn, and your legs feel like jelly, but you keep moving. You can barely see Musulin and Rajacich in the dark, but you can hear their heavy breathing.

Eventually, the sounds of the soldiers fade away. It's unbelievable that you all survived, but you did.

"That was close," Rajacich gasps when you finally stop for breath.

"Too close," Musulin replies, also breathing hard. "We'll have to be more careful."

For the next few weeks, you and your team travel from village to village, dodging

Turn the page.

German patrols and searching for trapped American crewmen. You find more than a dozen men scattered throughout the area.

You also gather intelligence from the villagers. They give you vital information about German troop locations and movements. This is exactly the kind of intel an OSS spy needs.

In one village, you discover a hidden radio. Excitedly, you make contact with the Cairo base. The next day, an Allied plane arrives to get you out. As you climb onboard, you think about everything that has happened. Even though you were forced to abandon Operation Halyard—for now—some men were saved. And you know you'll be back to get the rest.

THE END

To follow another path, turn to page 11.
To learn more about Operation Halyard, turn to page 103.

The villagers say the pilots who are hiding from the Nazis are safe and well cared for, so you decide to continue the Operation Halyard mission. The next morning, Nikola takes you to a Chetnik camp. The soldiers there are pleased to see you.

"Do you know anything about a large group of American pilots who are being sheltered by Yugoslavians?" Musulin asks.

"Yes of course," one soldier replies. "The American crewmen are gathered in Pranjani. It's a village about three days' travel away."

The Chetniks offer to take you to Pranjani. When you arrive, American soldiers enthusiastically greet you. Many of them have been trapped in Yugoslavia for weeks after their planes were shot down. They've been hiding in woods or villages and dodging German troops. Every day, Chetnik soldiers bring more downed American crewmen to the village.

Turn the page.

One day, a large group of Chetnik soldiers appear. They are led by the Yugoslavian army leader, Draza Mihailovic. Musulin embraces Mihailovic warmly.

George Musulin

The two leaders lay out the plan. The OSS and the U.S. Army will send cargo planes to rescue everyone. But you're worried.

"There are hundreds of Americans here," you say. "We won't be able to keep such a big rescue a secret from the Germans."

"We are getting everyone home," Musulin replies firmly. "The first thing we need to do is build an airstrip where the planes can land."

The villagers lead Musulin, Mihailovic, and a group of Chetnik and American crewmen to a large field halfway up a mountain. The land is uneven and covered with boulders. Here and there, cows are calmly grazing.

"It's not long enough," Rajacich says, looking worried. "Planes won't be able to land."

"It's our only option," Musulin replies. "We didn't know how many crewmen were stranded here until now—or exactly where they were. Now that we have that information, the only way to get all these men out quickly is to fly them out. And to do that, we need an airstrip."

You're astonished at this plan. How can anyone build a safe landing strip with no tools or equipment?

"Some groups will fill holes and smooth out the ground," Muslin continues. "Others will break up the boulders. There will be

Turn the page.

groups that will load wooden carts with debris and haul it away. Chetnik troops will patrol the area and keep us safe."

There's no way this will work. How can anyone keep such a huge project a secret? The Nazis are bound to figure it out sooner or later. When you tell Musulin about your worries, he nods in agreement.

"Yes, it's risky," he says. "More risky than I would like. But it is the only way to get everyone out fast. We won't leave one American behind. Now we need to contact base and tell them what we're doing. But as you know, we don't have a radio. I'm sending a team to scavenge plane wreckage for spare radio parts."

You could join the scavenging team. Or you could stick around and help build the airstrip.

To volunteer for the scavenging crew, go to page 67.

To volunteer to work on the airstrip, turn to page 70.

The next evening, you and the scavenging team set off. There are plenty of wrecked planes in the area, so you don't have a problem finding parts. You finally get everything you need—except one item.

"There are three downed planes farther away," one crewman says. "But they are close to a German patrol camp."

You can't build a radio without the part. "Let's go," you say.

Finally, you come upon the wreckage. Your heart sinks when you see it lies in the middle of a clearing. There's no cover, so you'll be exposed.

You carefully approach, all senses on alert. "Be ready to run," you whisper. "Your lives aren't worth a radio part."

As you get closer, German voices drift through the air, loudly singing. Hopefully, they're too busy having fun to notice you.

Turn the page.

You search the wreckage until you find the missing part. As you're climbing down, you lose your footing and fall into a pile of sharp, twisted metal. Without thinking, you yell in pain. The German singing stops, turning into shouts that move in your direction.

The wreckage of a B-29 bomber from WWII

The others frantically try to pull you out, but you can't move.

"Get out of here now," you hiss. Then you slump against the wreckage and play dead.

Several German soldiers appear, weapons drawn. One of them sees you and recoils in disgust, thinking you're a corpse. The others shake their heads and leave.

You wait until they're gone, then you raise your head. But you don't see the German soldier who stayed behind—or his knife. It only takes a few seconds for the world to go black.

THE END

To follow another path, turn to page 11.
To learn more about Operation Halyard, turn to page 103.

That evening, more than 100 Americans, villagers, and Chetnik soldiers trudge to the field. You break up boulders and load dirt and rocks onto wagons.

Six nights later, the airstrip is finished! The job that seemed impossible was completed in less than a week.

"We're not going to get everyone out at once," Musulin tells you. "We're only putting 12 men on each plane. This will keep the

The site of the evacuation airfield in Pranjani, located in present-day Serbia

weight down and allow the planes to take off on the short airstrip. If we tried to get everyone out, the Germans would see us. We're going to do it in small groups. The first planes will only take the injured and sick men."

You send the message that the airstrip is complete and ask for six rescue planes. That's enough to get the worst cases out quickly.

Immediately, a response comes through. The rescue is coming! Everyone is overjoyed. They're finally getting out.

The next night, you all gather at the airstrip. After a long wait, you hear the rumble of airplane engines.

The first plane swoops in to land. Right before it touches down, it abruptly pulls back up, turns around, and disappears into the dark.

You watch, feeling devastated. The airstrip is too short, and the plane can't land. There won't be a rescue tonight—or maybe ever.

Turn the page.

The disappointed men begin to head back to Pranjani. You're about to follow them when the second C-47 appears! You hold your breath as the plane touches down and races down the airstrip. It looks like it's going to crash into the mountain. Instead, it rolls to a stop.

The men cheer wildly as one by one, the other C-47s land. But there are only four C-47 cargo planes, not six.

Your stomach sinks. Why did they only send four? That means 24 sick and injured men won't be going home after all.

The pilots climb out and urge everyone to load as fast as possible.

"Where are the other two planes?" Musulin demands. "We asked for six, and there are only four!"

"Yes, sir," one pilot says. "The other two had engine trouble and couldn't make it. But we'll get these men out safely, sir, I guarantee it!"

Since there aren't enough planes, you decide to stay behind. There are others who are in more urgent need.

When the planes are loaded, the C-47 pilots wave to the crowd. "Don't worry, we're coming back!" they shout. Then, one by one, they take off and head back to safety.

You're disappointed that you didn't go. But you know they'll back, and soon you'll be headed home for good. Operation Halyard will be a succces.

THE END

To follow another path, turn to page 11.
To learn more about Operation Halyard, turn to page 103.

35
30
700
500
300
100
20
40
60
80
9
8
7
6
5
4
3
100%
80
100%
80

Chapter 4

RISKING EVERYTHING TO HELP THE AMERICANS

You grew up in a small mountain village in Yugoslavia. It was a quiet life with your family, and you were happy.

Then, in 1941, everything changed. Adolph Hitler ordered Nazi armies to conquer Yugoslavia. The small Yugoslavian army was no match for the powerful German forces and quickly surrendered.

But many Yugoslavian army officers and soldiers refused to give in. One of these officers was Draza Mihailovic. He formed an army of resistance fighters called Chetniks. When you heard Mihailovic wanted more soldiers, you leapt at the chance to join the Chetniks and defend your country.

Turn the page.

Now it's 1944. You're still a Chetnik soldier under Mihailovic's command—and Nazi toops still occupy your country.

One day Mihailovic gathers his Chetnik soldiers together.

"The Americans are attacking German oil refineries," he begins. "But the Luftwaffe shoots down many of their bombers. The

A German Luftwaffe fighter plane attacks an American bomber.

survivors often land here in Yugoslavia. I want you to be on the lookout for these Americans. If you find anyone, take them to the village of Pranjani. They will gather there and wait for rescue."

A few nights later, you are on a regular village patrol when German Luftwaffe attack a squad of American bombers right above you! The full moon lets you see several of the planes as they go down. Then, white parachutes appear in the sky. Some disappear into the forests to your right. Others float into a mountainous area to your left. You can't save both.

To go right, turn to page 78.

To go left, turn to page 88.

You cautiously make your way through the forest—this area is often patrolled by Germans. After some time, you spot a white parachute tangled high in the branches above you. Two Americans sit on the ground nearby.

"Who's there?" one says. He jumps to his feet, gun in hand.

You step out from the trees and hold out your empty hands. "Friend," you say in English. You're thankful that you've picked up enough English to be able to communicate with them.

The pilots relax. With a mix of hand motions and some words, they tell you the man on the ground has a badly broken leg. You communicate that there is a village nearby. They'll be safe there until they can travel to Pranjani, where more Americans are gathering.

You hoist the injured man onto your shoulders. The uninjured American gathers up their gear and follows.

American airmen hold a ripcord used to parachute into Yugoslavia before being rescued by Chetnik forces.

It's slow going, but you make it to the road. It is the fastest route to the village, but it also leaves you exposed, especially with the light from the full moon. German patrols might see you. You could continue through the forest, but it will take much longer, and this man needs help. Which route do you take?

To risk traveling along the road, turn to page 80.

To take the slow way through the forest, turn to page 85.

You decide to take the risk, so you follow the road. The injured man falls unconscious and gets heavier with each step. The other American tries to help, but he is weak and covered in bloody scratches.

You're only a mile or two away from the village, but you're exhausted and have to take a break. As you're sitting beside the road, you hear a rattling car engine from somewhere down the road.

You know that sound. It is a Kubelwagen, a German army jeep. It is likely filled with German soldiers—and it is approaching too fast for you to escape.

You hesitate. If you hide, the Germans might not see you—but you will lose the chance to attack. Confronting them surely means instant death. But it's a chance to stop them forever.

To hide beside the road, go to page 81.

To stay and fight, turn to page 83.

If the Germans spot you with the Americans, you're all dead. Together, you and the uninjured pilot drag the injured man into a ditch at the side of the road. Hopefully the Germans will miss you in the shadows.

From the ditch, you watch as the vehicle rounds a curve and heads toward you. Then the uninjured pilot gasps and touches your shoulder. His gear is piled up by the side of the road in plain sight. There is no way the Germans will miss it in the light of the moon. You hold your breath, afraid to see what happens next.

As the Kubelwagen drives past, one soldier shouts and points to the gear. The driver slams the brakes, and the jeep grinds to a stop. The soldiers jump out and grab the gear. Then they see you and freeze in surprise.

You freeze too. For a long moment, everyone simply stares at each other. Then,

Turn the page.

to your complete shock, the two Germans climb into their vehicle and drive away.

You can't believe they let you go. Why didn't they kill you? You make it to the village and tell the story of what happened. One older man pipes up.

"Those soldiers are just boys," he says dismissively. "Germany is so desperate for recruits that they force teenagers into the army. Those boys don't want to be here. They don't want to fight. You're lucky it was them who saw you."

Everyone agrees that this was the luckiest day for you all.

THE END

To follow another path, turn to page 11.
To learn more about Operation Halyard, turn to page 103.

You draw your weapon and duck behind some trees. The uninjured pilot drags his crewmate into the weeds, hoping to hide. The Kubelwagen passes and continues on. They didn't see you! You breathe a sigh of relief.

But as you walk out of the woods, the vehicle suddenly slams to a stop. Nazi soldiers jump out, guns in hand. You came out too quickly! They must have somehow seen your movements.

You aim your gun as they raise theirs. Before you can fire, several shots ring out from the weeds. The Nazis fall to the ground.

German soldiers ride in a Kubelwagen.

Turn the page.

The American pilot climbs out from the weeds, still holding his weapon. You are glad his aim was good.

The two of you load the unconscious pilot into the Kubelwagen and drive to the village, leaving the dead soldiers behind. The villagers assure you they will care for the American until he is healed enough to make it to Pranjani.

The uninjured American takes your hand in a firm handshake, his eyes bright with grateful tears. You shake his hand in return, happy you were able to help them get to safety.

Then, you drive the Kubelwagen back to your main camp. Mihailovic will be thrilled with such a prize! It will certainly come in handy to transport weapons and food to Chetnik camps.

THE END

To follow another path, turn to page 11.
To learn more about Operation Halyard, turn to page 103.

The forest is slower but safer, so you continue on. You struggle to navigate the thick forest while carrying the injured American, who is now unconscious.

For a time, the other pilot carries his friend, which helps. But eventually you must take a break. You gently lay the man down and gulp some water from your canteen.

Gunshots ring out through the trees. It's a German patrol!

The uninjured American quickly turns to you. "The Nazis will probably take us prisoner but let us live," he says. "But they have orders to kill any Yugoslavian who helps Americans. Get out of here while you can."

You understand most of what he says. Do you stay and fight or escape?

To stay, turn to page 86.

To escape, turn to page 87.

You won't abandon these men. But the choice will cost you. Seconds later, a squad of German soldiers bursts through the trees, shooting wildly. You feel a bullet rip through your side.

Clutching the wound, you collapse to the ground next to the unconscious American. The uninjured pilot keeps firing until he is shot as well.

You lay side by side as the Germans rush over. They stand over you, arguing back and forth. You're not sure what they're saying. All you can do is hope that the American and your family will survive the war, even though you will not.

THE END

To follow another path, turn to page 11.
To learn more about Operation Halyard, turn to page 103.

You dash into the thick underbrush to hide. Moments later, German soldiers, shouting and waving their weapons, rush through the trees. They head straight toward the Americans.

The uninjured pilot raises his hands above his head in surrender. One German grabs his hands and ties them. The other soldiers stand over the unconscious pilot. They argue for a moment before carrying out their decision. They search the dead man's body and take his weapons. Then they roughly take the other American away.

When they're gone, you emerge from your hiding place. You quietly take the dead pilot's dog tags from his neck. You'll give them to the next American you see. You may never know what happened to the American they took prisoner. But you can make sure *this* man's family knows what became of him.

THE END

To follow another path, turn to page 11.
To learn more about Operation Halyard, turn to page 103.

You climb the steep path to your left and find yourself in front of a small farm tucked into a mountain field. When you knock on the door, it flies open. Standing there is an American, guns aimed at your heart. Two more Americans are sitting at the rough wooden table.

A tiny Yugoslavian woman pushes the burly American aside and hugs you tightly.

“These men fell out of the sky!” she exclaims.

You learned some English from Mihailovic, so you are able to tell the Americans who you are. You also explain that you will take them to Pranjani, where other Americans have gathered. The woman is shocked to find out the Americans will be rescued.

The next morning, you lead them down the mountain. It's a five-day trip to Pranjani, but you make it without running into any Germans. The Americans are astounded at the number of men already here. They scatter to find their crewmates as Mihailovic sends for you.

"Three OSS officers arrived here yesterday," he says. "They are coordinating a huge rescue operation. They plan to fly all the men out."

"But how will they get everyone out without the Germans seeing them?" you ask.

"They don't expect to," Mihailovic replies. "They are sending fighter escorts to protect

Turn the page.

the rescue planes. But we have to build an airstrip so the rescue planes can land."

You stare at Mihailovic, shocked. How could anyone build an airstrip on the side of a mountain?

Before you can say anything, Mihailovic shakes his head. "Yes, these Americans have big ideas," he says. "But they manage to get most of them done. I trust they will be able to pull this one off too."

"There is much for us to do," Mihailovic continues. "Allies have dropped supply crates not far from here, and I need soldiers to pick them up. I also need men to set up guard posts outside the village."

To volunteer for guard duty, go to page 91.

To pick up the supplies, turn to page 93.

You join a group of Chetnik soldiers for night guard duty. They've set up posts around Pranjani to watch for Nazi patrols. You're assigned a large B-24 machine gun that was salvaged from a downed bomber. You set it up at a guard post on the main road to Pranjani. No German is going to get past you!

Around midnight, you hear a sound. Without warning, someone jumps you from behind. The cold steel of a German knife touches your neck. You roll out of the German soldier's grip and wrestle the knife from his hand.

The sound of fighting alerts the other Chetnik guards. They come running just as two more German soldiers appear out of the darkness. The quiet of the night is shattered by the sound of gunfire as the Chetniks and the Germans shoot at each other.

Turn the page.

The fight is over quickly. Fortunately, no one in your patrol is injured.

You make your report to Mihailovic the next day. He congratulates you and the other soldiers on your bravery.

"The airstrip is almost done," he adds. "Musulin has asked for some more Chetnik soldiers to help finish it. I also have a report of more Americans trapped in a village several miles from here."

Musulin is the leader of the Americans and a member of the OSS. He parachuted into Yugoslavia to organize the rescue. You would be honored to help him. But those Americans need to be brought to Pranjani before the rescue planes arrive.

To help with the airstrip, turn to page 94.

To get the trapped Americans, turn to page 96.

After dark, the group sets out to pick up supplies. The drop area is very close to enemy lines, so everyone is on high alert.

When you find the crates, everyone breaks them open and shoves supplies into their packs. You're almost done when you hear something in the woods. You motion for everyone to be quiet.

Slowly, you pull out your weapon. But before you can fire, *CRACK!* A shot rings out, and searing pain tears through your leg.

You fall to the ground. You know the bullet has hit an artery. You only have a few minutes left. Strangely, you're not afraid. Calmly, you close your eyes and think of your family as your mind goes dark.

THE END

To follow another path, turn to page 11.
To learn more about Operation Halyard, turn to page 103.

The airstrip is almost finished when you join the work crew. More than a hundred Americans and Yugoslavians have been working each night to get it done.

Someone hands you a hammer, and you break up boulders and rocks littering the field that will become the airstrip. Your hands are blistered and bloody from the rough tools. But no one dares stop.

It takes six days total to finsh the airstrip. Remarkably, the Germans don't discover it. Now it is time for the rescue that so many people worked so hard for.

The next night, hundreds of villagers, Chetniks, and Americans surround the airfield, nervously waiting. Will the planes really come?

In the distance, you hear the roar of an engine. A cheer goes up from the crowd as C-47 cargo planes come into view. But there are only four. That is not enough to transport all 500 Americans. Word spreads that they will send more planes soon, which is a relief.

When the planes land, you help load the injured pilots. To your surprise, one of them takes off his thick flight jacket and hands it to you. It is his way of saying thank you. You try it on, and it fits perfectly.

As the rescue planes—full of American soldiers—take off and disappear into the night, you feel grateful. The Americans are fighting in this war as hard as you are. With luck, you'll win.

THE END

To follow another path, turn to page 11.
To learn more about Operation Halyard, turn to page 103.

The village where the trapped Americans are hiding out is deep into German-held territory. It's going to be tough getting them out. You find four Chetnik soldiers who agree to go with you.

It's a three-day trip to the village by horseback, but it goes smoothly. When you arrive, the villagers greet you warmly. They take you to the homes where the Americans have been hiding.

Chetnik soldiers stand with an Italian officer (center).

You share that a huge rescue operation is in the works. The Americans are excited to hear it. You and the other soldiers decide to spend the night in the village and leave in the morning. That should give you enough time to get the Americans to Pranjani before the rescue planes arrive.

But the villagers have unsettling news. There have been rumors of German patrols destroying nearby villages. The Germans are known for this kind of cruelty. It might be a good idea to stay behind to defend the village. But the Americans need to get to Pranjani as fast as possible. What do you do?

To stay in the village, turn to page 98.

To lead the Americans to Pranjani, turn to page 100.

Two Chetniks agree to take the Americans to Pranjani. But someone needs to stay and protect the villagers. The other two soldiers volunteer to stay in the village with you.

"Flee if you can," you urge the villagers. "You need to get as far away from here as you can! I will stay behind until you are all safely away."

Fear is in the air as the villagers frantically gather their belongings and prepare to escape. You go from house to house, helping to gather supplies and load wagons. By midnight, many families are gone. But many others are still here.

The quiet of night is suddenly shattered by screams that echo in the air. German soldiers pour into the village. They quickly round up all the villagers and push you into a tight group. Then they throw bombs, setting everything on fire.

German soldiers fire an anti-tank gun during an attack on a Yugoslavian village.

Once the whole village is in flames, the soldiers surround the group and open fire. The scent of smoke and burning wood is the last thing you smell before death takes you.

THE END

To follow another path, turn to page 11.
To learn more about Operation Halyard, turn to page 103.

When you get to Pranjani, the rescue planes have already come and gone. The Americans are bitterly disappointed to learn they are too late, but Musulin assures them that more planes are coming.

The next day, the sky is filled with American planes. More than a dozen C-47 cargo planes land while a squad of fighter planes zooms toward nearby German camps. They will distract the Germans so the rescue planes can get away.

A few hours later, more rescue planes arrive. The crewmen that you rescued from the village find you. You are all overcome with emotion as they say goodbye. One gives you his warm leather flight jacket to thank you for saving their lives. It is all he has to give, and you are deeply grateful for his act of kindness.

Finally, all the Americans are in the planes. You watch the last C-47 take off, glad to

Allied airmen prepare to board a plane to evacuate from Yugoslavia.

have played a part in the rescue of so many Americans.

But you want to see your family. With Mihailovic's permission, you set out for your home village. World War II isn't over, but for now, your part in it is.

THE END

To follow another path, turn to page 11.
To learn more about Operation Halyard, turn to page 103.

Chapter 5

WHAT HAPPENED TO THE FORGOTTEN 500?

Operation Halyard was one of the biggest success stories of World War II. But almost no one knew it had ever happened. How could such an extraordinary mission be forgotten for so long?

At the time, the rescue was a top-secret operation. All the records about Operation Halyard were classified by the U.S. government. The soldiers who were rescued were ordered not to talk about it. It was not until the mid 1990s that the documents were declassified. By then, only a few people who remembered the mission were left.

One of those men was Arthur Jibilian. He served as an OSS secret agent and radio operator during Operation Halyard. During the rescue, he stayed behind in Pranjani, organizing communications until the last American left. After he was discharged from the army in 1945, Jibilian came home and built a life in Ohio. But he never forgot his experiences. When the mission documents were declassified, he began to tell his story. He shared photos that he took of the rescue.

The Operation Halyard memorial stands in the field where downed Allied airmen were rescued.

Clare Musgrove was another heroic survivor of Operation Halyard. He served as a gunner on a bomber that was shot down over Yugoslavia in the summer of 1944. He parachuted into a sheep field and was taken in by the sheep farmer and his family. Chetnik soldiers led him to the village of Pranjani, where he was airlifted to safety. Years later, Musgrove also started talking about Operation Halyard. Because of Jibilian, Musgrove, and other veterans, the story began to come to light.

In 2007, a book titled *The Forgotten 500: The Untold Story of the Men Who Risked All for the Greatest Rescue Mission of World War II* told the world about this incredible rescue mission. For the first time, the full story of Operation Halyard was revealed. The brave men who made it happen could finally get credit for their remarkable service.

MORE ABOUT THE RESCUE MISSION

- Operation Halyard was the largest rescue mission of WWII, but it almost didn't happen. It took many men and women to make the mission a reality, and many people played a role in its success.

- The Americans stranded in Nazi-occupied territories assumed their commanders had no idea they had survived being shot down and were trapped in Pranjani, Yugoslavia. So they decided to send a message to the U.S. base in Bari, Italy. They risked being found by the Nazis, but they decided to send it anyway.

- The stranded Americans asked Mihailovic to get them a radio, which he did. The first message they sent never got a reply. They decided to send a longer, coded message. This message gave their location and the number of men who were trapped. They added pilots' nicknames and the names of their bombers to the message. That way, the codebreakers at the base would know the message wasn't a German trick. They sent the message, hoping someone at the base would figure it out.

- Officers in Bari got the message and worked to break the code. After a couple of days, they did it! The commanders were excited and relieved to know their men were alive. Thanks to an OSS agent and his wife—George and Mirjana Vujnovich—they already knew about the stranded pilots and were working on a rescue plan. The information in the coded message was used by the OSS to parachute a team of agents to Pranjani and launch the rescue.

GEORGE AND MIRJANA VUJNOVICH

George Vujnovich was a member of the OSS stationed in Bari, Italy. His wife, Mirjana, worked at the Yugoslavian embassy in Washington, D.C. In May of 1944, the embassy received a letter from Mihailovic, telling them about the hundreds of American pilots stranded in Yugoslavia. No one paid attention to the letter—except Mirjana. She contacted George in Italy and told him about the letter and the trapped men. George took it seriously and soon confirmed it was true. He convinced the American commanders to create a rescue mission to save the men. Without George and Mirjana, Operation Halyard would never have taken place.

DRAZA MIHAILOVIC

One of the greatest heroes of Operation Halyard was Draza Mihailovic. His orders for Chetnik soldiers to find and rescue American servicemen allowed hundreds of men to survive. At first, U.S. military commanders considered him an ally. But rumors later spread that Mihailovic and his Chetnik forces were Nazi collaborators. Allied commanders abandoned Mihailovic. After the war, Josip Tito—the Communist leader of Yugoslavia—had Mihailovic arrested and tried for treason. Mihailovic was executed in Yugoslavia in 1946.

The Operation Halyard survivors who knew Mihailovic were outraged. They knew Mihailovic was not a traitor. Some of the American veterans went to Yugoslavia during Mihailovic's trial for support. Others wrote to U.S. newspapers to clear his name. Eventually, the U.S. government admitted they had been wrong. President Harry S. Truman even awarded Mihailovic the Legion of Merit after he was executed. It is the highest U.S. honor given to a foreign national. But Operation Halyard stayed a secret, and the award was given the same way. Finally, on May 9, 2005, the award was publicly presented to Mihailovic's daughter, Gordana.

KEY MISSION EQUIPMENT

C-47 cargo planes were used to airlift Allied airmen out of Nazi-occupied Yugoslavia during Operation Halyard.

Evacuated American airmen keep their feet warm in special bags after giving their shoes to the Yugoslavian people who helped them.

RESCUE TIMELINE

FALL 1943—Allied forces occupy Italy and begin planning missions to destroy Nazi oil refineries in Romania.

JANUARY 1944—The first Americans are shot down over Yugoslavia during bombing raids on oil refineries. Yugoslavian Army leader Draza Mihailovic is notified. Mihailovic orders the Chetnik army to rescue any downed airmen they find.

MAY 1944—Mirjana Vujnovich hears rumors of 100 downed pilots trapped in Yugoslavia. She passes this information to her husband, George Vujnovich. He and others ask U.S. President Franklin Roosevelt for permission to mount a rescue.

JULY 1944—Downed American airmen establish radio contact with U.S. forces. President Roosevelt approves an OSS mission to send three agents into Yugoslavia to find the trapped airmen and organize a rescue mission.

AUGUST 1944—The OSS team arrives in Pranjani, Yugoslavia, and discovers more than 400 Americans needing rescue. Construction of the airstrip is completed in six days. The OSS team contacts the U.S. Army to send six rescue aircraft.

AUGUST 9–10, 1944—Four C-47 cargo airplanes arrive and evacuate the first group of American airmen.

AUGUST 12, 15, 18, 1944—Three more rescue missions evacuate the rest of the trapped Americans.

DECEMBER 1944—Operation Halyard is officially closed. More than 500 Americans were rescued during the operation.

MARCH 1946—Mihailovic is arrested by Yugoslavian Communist leader Josip Tito and put on trial for treason.

JULY 1946—Mihailovic is executed.

MARCH 29, 1948—U.S. President Harry S. Truman awards Mihailovic the Legion of Merit.

GLOSSARY

airstrip (AIR-strip)—a runway without normal air base or airport facilities

bombardier (bahm-buh-DEER)—a bombing crew member who controls where and when bombs drop from airplanes

canteen (kan-TEEN)—a small metal container for holding water

classified (KLAH-suh-fide)—top secret

code (KOHD)—a system of letters, symbols, and numbers used to send secret messages

evacuate (i-VA-kyuh-wayt)—to leave an area during a time of danger to go somewhere safer

Luftwaffe (LOOFT-vahf-uh)—the German air force

navigator (NAV-uh-gay-tuhr)—someone who plans an airplane's flight path; navigators read maps for pilots

Nazi (NOT-see)—a member of a political party led by Adolf Hitler; the Nazis ruled Germany from 1933 to 1945

parachute (PAIR-uh-shoot)—a large piece of strong, lightweight fabric; parachutes allow people to jump from high places and float slowly and safely to the ground

patrol (puh-TROHL)—a person or group that guards an area

refinery (ri-FAHY-nuh-ree)—a place where petroleum is made into gasoline, motor oil, and other products

salvage (SAL-vij)—the act of saving something from damage or waste

READ MORE

Halls, Kelly Milner. *World War II History for Kids: 500 Facts*. New York: Callisto Kids, 2021.

Roman, Carol. *Spies, Codebreakers, and Secret Agents: A World War II Book for Kids (Spies in History for Kids)*. New York: Callisto Kids, 2020.

INTERNET SITES

Imperial War Museums
iwm.org.uk

National Museum of World War II Aviation
worldwariiaviation.org

National World War II Museum
nationalww2museum.org

ABOUT THE AUTHOR

Allison Lassieur loves to write books about real things, and she's very happy you've picked this book to read. She's written more than 150 nonfiction books about everything from medieval knights to the Loch Ness monster. (Okay, Nessie probably isn't real, but it was fun to write about her anyway.) When she's not researching a book or writing one, Allison likes to read, knit, and eat chocolate cake. She lives in a very old house in upstate New York with her daughter, a sweet, silly dog, and more books than she can count.

MORE BOOKS IN THIS SERIES

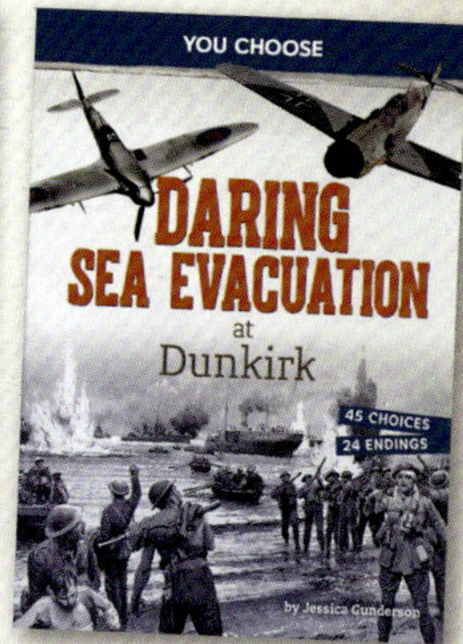